The

Church

at

Auroraville

An Historical Narrative
1918 - 1946

Library of Congress Control Number 2010942833
ISBN 978-1-4507-5409-5

To purchase this book, contact:

Valerie Ann Demos
WEC-FMD
8855 Dunn Road
Hazelwood, MO 63042
ALDemos@aol.com

Printed in the United States of America by
Dimension Printing
Sarasota, Florida

The Church at Auroraville

The story of
witnesses
who inspired many
to seek salvation
through a church
in a quiet farmland village
in central Wisconsin
in the early 1900s

A tribute to
faith
fidelity
fortitude

A loving acknowledgement of
the pioneers of Pentecost

Jon Hardt, Author
Valerie Demos, Editor

The Church at Auroraville
1927

CONTENTS

The white circle is the approximate area which *The Church at Auroraville* served. Auroaville is just off Highway 21 about 25 miles west of Oshkosh, Wisconsin.

Folks from villages around, with names like Poy Sippi, Redgranite, Omro, Pine River, Ripon, Green Lake, Berlin, Eureka, Picket, Germania and Waukau, came to Auroraville and found salvation.

Where is Auroraville?

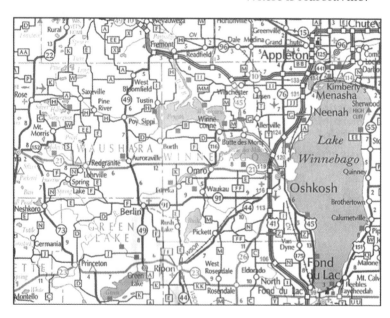

ACKNOWLEDGEMENTS

We wish to acknowledge all pioneer pastors and evangelists for their sacrifices and perseverance in the early 1900s. Churches rose up all across America because of these early efforts. Each church merits the same honor, respect and gratitude that this book intends to bring to the leaders and members of *The Church at Auroraville.*

Some such churches are still active, others consolidated, some now only memories. Still, all were singular forces in establishing the apostolic Pentecostal movement in their part of the world. We could and, perhaps, should place a monument at each site where a church once stood, inscribed with words befitting the tribute each deserves.

The Wisconsin village of Auroraville was a small farmland community of about one hundred people when our story began to unfold. It developed around a stream that powered a gristmill that ground the feed for area farmers' livestock. It was an unlikely setting from which a lively Pentecostal church would emerge, but emerge it did.

Our intriguing tale centers around two compelling witnesses – a blood brother and sister – and all those who became their brothers and sisters in Christ. The brother, Carl Frederick Ebert, and his wife led the way boldly into the faith and he introduced his sister, Rosa Ebert Oelke, to Pentecost soon afterward. She went on to win other family members and her circle of influence widened quickly to include countless friends and neighbors. These believers would go on to build and pay for a church building in Auroraville in some of the worst economic times in America. Hundreds would come through its doors to find salvation at its altar and go out to share the "wonderful words of life" with many more.

It can be said of all those who claim Auroraville as their spiritual birthplace that they used meager means to produce rich results. *The Church at Auroraville* was notable for spreading Pentecost throughout east central Wisconsin, resulting in the foundation of several area churches. In addition, families that were rooted and grounded in this Pentecostal way through that village church were predecessors to many who faithfully carry on the work of the ministry around the world to this day.

For these reasons, we relish the opportunity to recognize those we know by name who gave financially, physically and spiritually to establish and pass along the message of Pentecost in the early 1900s in Wisconsin. These, and all others, whose names we have not heard or have not had occasion to mention, will gather together in eternity to be recognized fully by God Almighty. We will have opportunity then and there to rejoice and be thankful because of the great things He did to enrich our lives through these notable pioneers in the Upper Midwest.

INTRODUCTION

AZUSA TO AURORAVILLE

The dramatic story of Auroraville fits into the larger phenomenon recorded in church history as a restoration of Pentecost. Scholars can point to several momentous events happening around the world at the turn of the century that contributed to this renewal but there is no doubt that spiritual manifestations in America and Canada were among the most spectacular and enduring of all. The historic revival on Azusa Street in Los Angeles, California that broke out in 1906 would propel the Pentecostal movement from a few isolated believers to a force of respect and significance within Christianity.

The news of happenings on Azusa Street spread like wild fire. People came from all over America and from abroad to witness the outpouring of the Holy Ghost.[1] They returned home to explain what they themselves had experienced or had seen happening to many others. Soon, thousands around the world were experiencing their own Pentecost. By 1914, organized structures were in place in America to assist existing churches in transition and to support a rising number of new Pentecostal groups. The Assemblies of God, Pentecostal Assemblies of the World and Pentecostal Ministerial Alliance were among the most prominent organizations of the times. Additional shifts occurred later in these and other church bodies in order to safeguard the restoration of apostolic doctrine, concluding

[1] The term *Holy Ghost* is synonymous with the term *Holy Spirit*. In the King James English Bible, *Holy Spirit* is found just seven times, three times in the Old Testament and four times in the New Testament. By contrast, *Holy Ghost* appears ninety times in the New Testament, not being used in the Old Testament at all. A reference, "poured out the gift of the Holy Ghost," can be found in Acts 10:45.

with the merger of two separate apostolic groups in 1945 to form the United Pentecostal Church.

Andrew D. Urshan, an Assyrian immigrant, was swept into the revival of the times and was a ministering member of the three organized bodies mentioned above, moving eventually into the United Pentecostal Church.[2] He became an articulate spokesman for the rebirth of apostolic Pentecostalism throughout his many years of amazing ministry. With headquarters in Chicago, Illinois, he evangelized in Canada, throughout the Midwest and in other countries, including Iran and Russia; he also pastored churches, including Midway Tabernacle in St. Paul, Minnesota from 1920-21. His impact on various assemblies as well as upon indigenous groups of people was enormous and enduring.

As for Wisconsin, God chose to bring attention to a small village, located about a hundred miles north and slightly west of Milwaukee, nestled in the middle of scenic farmland. It had originally been named Daniel's Mills because of the grist and lumber mills on location. Later, the female residents thought it better to use the name *Aurora*, which means *"a new beginning."* When they discovered that other nearby communities had already taken that name, they settled on calling their village *Auroraville*, which would mean *"the place of new beginnings."* This choice became prophetic as hundreds of people were born again of the water and the Spirit along a seemingly insignificant country road!

The village was built next to a dam on Willow Creek that formed a large lake the locals called the millpond. It provided water and power to operate the mills, the principle economy and attraction of Auroraville. The area

---

[2] The U.P.C. eventually adopted the name of *United Pentecostal Church International* (U.P.C.I.) and will be so referenced further.

around the millpond became a natural gathering place for residents and visitors alike who first attended to farm business and, then, lingered awhile for leisurely visits and some shopping. In time, many of these same folks would gather at the old millpond for a higher purpose, a sacred purpose, i.e., for baptisms.

Auroraville was a sleepy village, by all accounts. Only one church, a Methodist church, existed to serve the people's spiritual interests. The low attendance indicated that there really wasn't much interest in Christianity until the Pentecostal fire began to fall all around the village. A great spiritual awakening would eventually turn the village into a vibrant center of evangelism.

The tiny and picturesque village of Auroraville - circa 1918
The large cheese factory at the far left would become
The Church at Auroraville.
Ahead of the wagons is a bridge built over the millpond spillway.
The dark building to the right of the bridge is a mill.

The Church at Auroraville was never going to be about the three buildings used during its lifetime or about any of the prominent people in Pentecost who would flock to its gatherings. The focus would always be on spreading the apostolic message and allowing the Holy Ghost to move and linger in every gathering. This church accomplished amazing things under strenuous circumstances in a relatively short period of time. Its history began to build spontaneously after a series of normal events brought people face to face with opportunities to hear the Gospel and receive the promise of the Father, also called the gift of the Holy Spirit, through faith in Jesus Christ, our Lord.

Chapter One

A BURNING WITNESS

The Auroraville church fulfilled many interesting purposes during its lifetime. It hosted ministerial conferences, divine-healing campaigns and minister-training seminars for the entire upper Midwest. Locally, it was a place of deliverance, healing, salvation and fellowship. The inspiration for this book did not come from the preachers, teachers, leaders or exciting events of the time but rather from the humble beginnings of the church. Particularly, one woman held the future of revival in east central Wisconsin in her heart and hands and handled it with excellence.

Rosa (Rose) Ebert Oelke

In the early 1900s, there were probably no better places in which to live and grow up than areas around Green Lake, Wisconsin, a prosperous and popular resort town. Three youngsters, Carl, Rosa and Lydia Ebert, born before the turn of the century, grew up on a farm not far from Green Lake. God had them in His sights, it seems, long before they ever knew they would become vessels of honor in the Kingdom of God. In fact, this man and his two sisters were well into their marriages before the windows of heaven opened and God's power was poured out on each family unit. Once these siblings and their spouses heard, believed and experienced the message of Pentecost, they could not and would not keep it quiet.

Carl learned farming from his father and also skills in carpentry and building construction. He had a great start on the road to becoming a successful entrepreneur. He married Martha Frank and they eventually parented three daughters. Rosa, his sister, who had blossomed into a fine young lady, caught the eye of Edward Oelke, a man with farming and carpentry skills equal to his future brother-in-law. Lydia married William Rayback, another excellent carpenter. The men in this extended family must have spent a great deal of time helping each other sharpen the tools of the trade!

Living had to be good for the married Ebert clan during the time they all lived in Green Lake and could routinely enjoy one another's company. When Carl decided to move his immediate family elsewhere, he unwittingly opened the door for change from a good life to an abundant life. Before the Eberts hardly had time to miss one another, they were walking together again down a new and very different pathway.

Carl's reason for moving was rooted in the idea that a rather prominent city in west central Wisconsin held more promise for successful business ventures than did Green

Lake. Sometime after 1915, he relocated his family to Eau Claire when the automobile industry was growing and creating jobs. The thought was that people working good jobs would be in the market for new housing. Carl definitely knew how to build nice homes and had no problem finding buyers in Eau Claire. Given the economics of that time and place, his skill as a builder and contractor would probably have led Carl to considerable wealth. As it turned out, the family did become rich but not necessarily in earthly goods.

Carl opened a confectionary store in a downtown Eau Claire hotel to secure a second source of income and put Martha basically in charge while he searched for home-building opportunities.   One day, a wonderful thing happened at the candy store. As usual, Martha was running it alone and two men came in with invitations to a local Pentecostal gathering. They carried a sign that advertised a series of tent meetings and politely asked if they might put it in her store window. Martha obliged and she was probably the first one to take a personal interest in the advertised event. She had been to various outdoor

Carl Frederick Ebert

meetings before but had never heard of Pentecost. Her curiosity and hunger for the Lord was so great that she launched an investigation completely on her own. She went to the first meeting without Carl, having no clue that she was about to set a powerful spiritual progression into motion. Martha was deeply moved by what she saw and heard; she could hardly wait to go back! The joy those Pentecostal tent worshippers exhibited in the presence of the Lord captivated her soul and she longed to have that same "joy unspeakable and full of glory!"

She went home to share her best understanding with Carl about what she had learned, suggesting that he join her at a later meeting. Given that Martha was impressed, he was willing to check things out. They began to attend the meetings together and realized shortly that something of importance for salvation had come their way. After some serious considerations and careful examinations, husband and wife were both convinced about the value and validity of the Pentecostal message.

Once they were baptized and filled with the Holy Ghost, all previous ambitions and dreams came under submission to the will of God for the Ebert family. Carl made a pledge to preach the Gospel if only God would heal his baby girl, Eunice, who was gravely ill. God healed Eunice and her daddy became a preacher.

Carl and Martha went forward and brought forth much fruit to the glory and honor of their Lord. All who knew of Carl's exploits considered him a hero of the faith but fewer realized that his wife was a woman equally worthy of fond recollection. Her immediate family adored her and, as another relative put it, one *"could see the face of Jesus in her when she testified. She was a gracious, saintly woman who wrote compelling letters about the Oneness nature of God."* [3]

In the year 1919, soon after the Eberts had come into Pentecost, Rosa Oelke came for a friendly visit from Green Lake, not knowing that she would land right in the middle of Eau Claire Pentecostal enthusiasm. She realized almost

---

[3] Recollection – Marjorie Burns Oelke, as told to her daughter, Mary Oelke Geissler, granddaughter to Rose Oelke

immediately that what was transpiring in the lives of her beloved brother and sister-in-law was something wonderful. She studied the Bible in order to substantiate what they were telling her and was caught up in a whirlwind of new ways of thinking and living that would require some thorough and single-handed explanations when she got back home.

In the meantime, she participated in a landmark church called Pentecostal Assembly that was in its formative stages in Eau Claire. Joseph Rulien, a local Swedish fellow, was one of the leaders. In search of his own spiritual satisfaction, he had traveled to Topeka, Kansas in 1906 where he received the Holy Ghost.

By 1918, back in Eau Claire, Joseph was holding house meetings and was voted in as pastor of Pentecostal Assembly when the growing group incorporated as a church in 1920. He remained in that position until his death in 1952. During these years of ministry in Wisconsin, it was said that he *"wielded much power as he was so anointed and had so much*

Pastor Joseph Rulien

compassion." Others remember that he normally spoke with a heavy Swedish brogue but his words would come out in unaccented English when speaking in the church.

Joseph Rulien is known to have participated in a tent revival in the midway section of St. Paul, Minnesota that was continuous from 1915-1917. Consensus has it that those tent meetings launched Midway Tabernacle. Prominent preachers in St. Paul, some with connections to Azusa Street, also ministered in Eau Claire and were probably the ones who organized the tent meetings that brought Carl and Martha Ebert into the faith.

By the time Rosa pulled herself away from the nurturing spiritual atmosphere in Eau Claire, she had come to grips with her situation. Any fear to face the reality back home was obviously quelled by a determination to change it and take the upper hand in her circumstances. Instead of letting her fledgling faith shrivel up and die, she resolved to round up some spiritual companionship to help keep it alive. Like the faithful ones rewarded in the parable of the talents, she chose to invest and multiply her treasure rather than hide it.

Definitely a novice in the art of evangelism and the knowledge of the Word, her testimony must have been greatly anointed because people listened to her! Of course, the first ones to hear the revolutionary news were her family members. Her husband appears to have been somewhat skeptical or, at least, reserved about accepting the Gospel when he first heard it but as Rosa began to invite her neighbors in for Bible studies, he did not hinder her. In the end, her persistence broke down his resistance and they became equal partners in a steady stream of wonderful witnessing endeavors.

Rosa's sister, Lydia, was an instant believer. She saw a great change for good in her sister and wanted the same for herself. She became a student of the scriptures so she could explain to her good husband, William Rayback, how important it was for them to trust and obey. They came into the faith together and lived faithfully for God all the rest of their lives, William offering his carpentry skills to benefit churches throughout the years.

By default, the Oelke residence turned into a center of communication for the Pentecostal message in the Green Lake area. Interest ran high and a probable question floating around town was, "Have you heard about what's going on over at Rose's home?" Bible studies and prayer meetings were ongoing, whether scheduled or occurring spontaneously. Silver Creek ran conveniently behind the house and was just what the Bible ordered - a natural baptistery. The regular spectacle of creek water used for a holy purpose became a witness all its own. More and more folks stopped by with questions and stayed around for the meetings. Rosa was on a roll!

Rose, Reuben, Jimmy and Edward Oelke

Someone invited a fellow named Fredric Welk, a road-building contractor, to the Oelke house meetings. No one seems to know whether he personally became a believer or not, but something motivated him to encourage others to check into the curious happenings in Green Lake. He was in charge of new road construction between the towns of

Berlin and Green Lake and his crew ended up working on a road that ran right in front of the Fred and Pauline Lentz farm. One fine day during a lunch or coffee break, perhaps, Fred Lentz walked out of his house, intending to ask the men how the job was going. Instead, his attention was drawn to an entirely different topic. He got to the group just in time to hear Fredric coaxing his crew to attend the Oelke house meetings. Fred probably took them all by surprise when he was the one to ask for directions! Fredric explained how to get there and even suggested that Fred take his wife along.

Fred did Fredric one better and took his two daughters as well as his wife. It was the start of a full family involvement that favored its members for all the years they would live. The four Lentz family members were baptized together in Silver Creek and the two young daughters, Alice and Esther, along with their parents, would prove to be great assets in the Kingdom of God.

Fred and Pauline Lentz

Fred was a gregarious fellow and managed to slip a key question into conversations with just about everyone. "Have you heard about Pentecost?" He brought scores of people into the church at a remarkable rate. His first convert was Billy Page, a young farm hand he had hired. Fred invited him one day to join in an Oelke house meeting and everyone was delighted by his response. He not only attended but also responded wholeheartedly. Subsequently, he wasted no time in reaching out to his own friends and family. The number of new converts swelled as one witness led to another and, then, to another.

Back at the Lentz home, Fred and Pauline needed some new kitchen cabinets in their farmhouse. They hired Charles Dunham, a carpenter living in the neighboring town of Berlin, to do this work. While on the job, Fred began to tell Charles about his spiritual transformation and mentioned that regular meetings were being held over in Green Lake. As usual, Fred's gift of friendly persuasion worked its magic. Carpenter Dunham and his wife, Emily, a schoolteacher by profession, went off to Green Lake to probe into Pentecost.

These two newcomers from Berlin must have liked what they learned because soon they had joined the many others who were being baptized in Silver Creek. Emily designed Bible classes just for children and blessed church families with this ministry for many, many years. Charles joined the ranks of the skilled carpenters in the church and generously lent his skills to countless building projects. Charley, as he preferred to be called, was not a preacher or a teacher. He had

Charles and Emily Dunham

the gift of helps, an essential ingredient in the success of any church body. Many preachers, pastors and people were thankful to have this fine couple at work within the fellowship that kept growing steadily through spontaneous witnessing.

The Dunhams were responsible for bringing their neighbors John and Ida Jordan into the church. Ida was a sister to Fred Lentz and she knew that his family had taken on a new way of life. He tried to explain the spiritual motivation behind the changes but Ida wasn't listening very well. God had to plant a more palatable witness right in Ida's back yard. When Ida realized that neighbors were taking the same religious direction as relatives, her ears apparently perked up. She and John were soundly converted and a new preaching point opened under the lay ministries of the Dunham and Jordan families.

John passed away not long after he and his wife came into Pentecost, but Ida graciously kept her home open to meetings for outreach and teaching. Ida later married a man named Fred Schmid who became a wonderful husband and fine father to her two children. Fred would later lend his business expertise to *The Church at Auroraville* by serving for years as the trusty church bookkeeper. Much later, Ida's son Herbert would marry Ferinda, the eldest of three daughters born to Carl and Martha Ebert.[4]

Another soul-winning venture that should be mentioned before we close this chapter of beginnings puts a particularly fine feather in Fred's cap. Fred had met Joseph Elstad, a linotype operator for the Berlin newspaper, and, of course, talked about the Lord with him. The entire Elstad family gladly received the Word and Joseph became a masterful communicator of the Gospel. He would go on to serve *The Church at Auroraville* as pastor, one in a long list of men who provided sound doctrinal teaching for the church.

Fred and Pauline Lentz spent a lifetime spreading the message of Pentecost. They won key people to the Lord who furthered the Gospel in the same spirit that they embodied. Reflecting back on that chance conversation with a road contractor, who seemed to have no personal interest in the Gospel, Fred always characterized it as a divine intervention that turned his life into an unimaginable and privileged new direction.

---

[4] An abbreviated family tree appears in Chapter Twelve.

The Church at Auroraville

Chapter Two

BEYOND ROSA

The Oelke family residency in Green Lake was one of those good things that had to come to an end. Demand for new homes in that part of Wisconsin was subsiding. By contrast, the Eau Claire building business, hinged to the thriving auto industry, was still strident. Carl convinced Edward to take advantage of the greater prosperity he was experiencing further north. For these long-term residents in Green Lake, such a major move would not be easy. First of all, they would be leaving a home, friends and family of many years. Furthermore they would be creating a vacuum in the leadership of the burgeoning church.

The decision to pull up stakes came after much prayer, realizing that the scattered groups of faithful followers would likely flounder while adjusting to the loss of leadership. Many men had come periodically to minister in the home groups, including Rosa's own energetic brother Carl, but none of them could stay on to take responsibility for the flock. The welfare of the church people was foremost in the minds of the Edward Oelke family as they formulated plans to relocate in Eau Claire.

When Rosa left her country life for city life in Eau Claire, her love for the Word and desire to be a witness did not wane. She became a mentor, an inspiration and a staunch proponent of the doctrines of the church at Pentecostal Assembly. She lived out her long life never perceiving, perhaps, her true value as a facilitator for revival.

As for those she left behind in Green Lake, everything was under God's control. The situation might be compared, in reverse, to the persecution in Jerusalem that forced the early Christians to scatter. The negative pressure then became the positive impetus for church growth outside of the city. The departure of the Oelke family, while definitely a loss, pressed the people to come together and ultimately resulted in greater church growth within the village. Our God always knows how to turn a bad situation into something good. He would do it often for these people, in dramatic ways, as they learned how to trust completely in Him.

Faithful followers had already begun to meet challenges before Rosa's family moved away. Other homes had opened for various kinds of meetings, adding convenience for those who had been traveling long distances to the Oelke home. This arrangement was effective until such a time as the size of the groups and the need for systematic teaching called for a fixed place of worship in an accessible central location.

When that time came, the group leaders sat down with a map, pinpointed the location of each home group and decided on the most convenient location for organizing into one church body. Auroraville was the clear choice and the rest is history. A former general store building was vacant just west of the village and, before the residents knew what was happening, a new church had appeared on the edge of town! It was not a large facility but it served to get the meetings out of the homes. The first apostolic church in east central Wisconsin, *The Church at Auroraville*, was up and running.

The final step in transitioning from home meetings to church meetings would be the most daunting of all. The sheep needed a shepherd for their care and feeding, a designated pastor to lead them as a more formal congregation. The majority of "the sheep" were farmers and this posed an economic problem.

It was the early 1920s when some sectors of society in America were experiencing an economic boom. Unfortunately, it was not so for the farmers.

Summer Bible Studies in the early 1920s

What could a band of struggling farmers assuredly offer to a prospective pastor when their own income was below par?

All they had was a small store building for a worship center with a large number of exuberant people scattered around outside the village. Not to be intimidated, the people mobilized their faith in prayer for a miracle, knowing the times were working against them but God was working for them. They needed a pastor and soon would need a better facility as well. The Lord graciously provided both.

The church growth brought exhilaration on one hand and consternation on the other. The general store had solved one set of problems but was quickly becoming a problem of its own. It was simply not big enough for the increasing attendance. Around the bend from this desperate situation was another building waiting just for them. It had been built as a hotel that eventually became a cheese factory. When the cheese makers vacated, this building presented the perfect possibility for a spacious and suitable house of worship right in the heart of the village.

The several skilled carpenters in the group brainstormed and concluded that they could turn the first floor of the plant into a spacious sanctuary. The same astute men carefully examined the residual hotel rooms on the top floor and figured out how to turn them into sizeable living quarters. They concurred that, given a complete facelift, this former cheese factory could become everything and more than the believers needed at the time. The church leaders made an agreement to rent the old cheese factory and the carpenters pooled their tools and went into action. When the renovation was finished, the people were ecstatic because they finally had something appropriate to offer a preacher and his family in exchange for sound spiritual leadership in Auroraville. The diligent Pentecostal people in the village took great pride in what they had already achieved and all that remained was to find a parson for the parsonage!

A photo from the times [page 26] shows a sign above the church entrance that can barely be read but reveals an official name for the church, i.e., Pentecostal Assembly. The name was borrowed, no doubt, from the sister congregation in Eau Claire. Interestingly, *The Church at Auroraville* would take on an informal name as well, coined by the townspeople but accepted by the church people. It would become known affectionately as the "cheese factory" church.

Never mind! Those who went inside and stayed awhile learned the truth about what was available behind closed doors. The stock supplies were the Bread of Life and the Honey in the Rock, along with the Milk and the Meat of the Word. The only cheese to be found was, no doubt, in the delicious food prepared by the women for times of fellowship. In this particular "cheese factory," people tasted and found that the LORD was good.

Willow Creek
Ground hallowed by countless baptisms

Some of the congregation at the "cheese factory" church - circa 1924

Ida Jordan, *1st left* - **Fred Lentz**, *5th right* - **Billy Page**, *2nd right*

The Church at Auroraville

Chapter Three

FIRST PASTOR

Carl Trittin was a quiet and scholarly gentleman called to teach rather than preach. God used him to bring understanding about that which scores of people were experiencing, particularly the rationale for baptism in the Name of Jesus and the infilling of the Holy Spirit. He lived in Appleton, Wisconsin with his large family but was willing to travel out to conduct seminars for days at a time in response to frequent requests. He gave himself unselfishly to the work of the ministry. Many of the early apostolic churches throughout the Midwest would attribute their solid spiritual foundation to the teaching of this itinerate man of God.

Teacher Carl Trittin

Carl was aware that the ever-expanding Auroraville assembly needed a pastor yet felt it was not God's will for him to meet the need directly. In caring fashion, he let the church know that he would be praying with them and keeping an eye out for potential pastors. As a traveling teacher, he was connected to a network of Pentecostals and he, if anyone, could discover who was available.

Around 1919, two young people, Reinhold Sass and Lydia Minikel, met in the Church of God in Milwaukee, Wisconsin and a mutual life experience drew them together. They were both immigrants of German descent.

When they decided to marry, they made plans to take a honeymoon trip to Indianapolis, Indiana.

G. T. Haywood, a songwriter and preacher of considerable renown in apostolic Pentecostal circles, had a thriving church in Indianapolis that the young couple visited while in town. A wonderful unexpected thing happened to them

Reinhold and Lydia Sass

on the way through a honeymoon. They came face to face with discussions about the various formulas being used in water baptism. Reinhold was delighted to hear and learn more on this topic. While living in Michigan, he had been introduced to the subject and became convinced that the rite of baptism was to be performed in the Name of Jesus. He had been so baptized there but had not yet broached the subject with Lydia. When she heard about it first in Indianapolis, he offered his own opinion that the teaching was correct, having high hopes that there would be no disagreement on the matter.

Can you imagine their added sense of fulfillment when Lydia gladly received this teaching? It was February of 1920 when she was buried with Christ in baptism. Oh, what a honeymoon they were having in Indianapolis! And, that's not all. Another person from Wisconsin was visiting the Haywood church at that very time and the Wisconsinites were drawn to each other. It was Carl Trittin, the man on the move. This meeting forged a life-long relationship between the two men and their families. Carl began mentoring the young couple, creating in them a hunger to be students of the Scriptures. He must have done his job well because Reinhold and Lydia Sass became known for their Bible knowledge and ability to teach others in the same fashion as they had been taught.

Just after the honeymoon, back in Milwaukee, reality set in and brought this new husband and wife considerable disappointment. They could not find an apostolic Pentecost church anywhere in the city. In time, they would solve that problem but, first, they had to learn some things in the school of hard knocks. The lessons learned from Carl Trittin were indispensible but training of another kind would come through harrowing experiences.

Reinhold believed, initially, that he had a missionary call to reach his German family and friends. He was actually a German-Russian[5] whose relatives were among those living in German enclaves within Russia. Reinhold felt that he and Lydia had an innate understanding of how to reach the "GR" people with the Gospel and they were willing to sacrifice the greater comforts and conveniences of America in order to take the Gospel abroad to their own people.

Collecting funds for a missionary journey was no easy task but they began in earnest, traveling from one church or home group to another, carrying all their personal belongings in a car. Months into the journey, they were stunned by the theft of their vehicle. Emotionally shattered and completely broke, this couple pressed on in Jesus' Name. They were bent on being useful wherever and whenever God would open the door. Thwarted

---

[5] commonly referred to as a "GR" person

financially, they were somewhat comforted to learn that they were not the only ones in trouble. The Russian government was in political turmoil and there was a famine in the land.[6] It was not a time when foreigners could expect to get residency and sustain a living in that part of the world. Interestingly, the door to Russia did not open for Reinhold and Lydia any time later. Instead, the Lord had much for them to do in America.

In the midst of uncertainty, Reinhold and Lydia were always lifted up by one sure thing. The Sass and Trittin friendship was firmly in place and the younger ones felt a great sense of security under the wing of their mentor. Accepting advice from Elder Trittin, Reinhold and Lydia began to use their growing teaching skills to focus on conducting services at home in Milwaukee. At the same time, they were building up personal resources for a time when they might sense the Lord calling them to work in a field away from home. They wanted to be ready to go.

Carl Trittin had often ministered in and around Auroraville in the early days of house meetings and even after the development of a standing congregation. Off and on, he would invite Reinhold to join him and this early relationship with the Auroraville believers set the stage for a more substantial collaboration down the line.

On one of Carl's frequent visits to Milwaukee, Reinhold mentioned that he would like to develop his ministry further by working as an understudy with a pastor. Up to that time, no apostolic Bible schools had been established in America and, for that reason, on-the-job training was the only real option for those called to the ministry. Reinhold was willing to leave the security of home for the greater goal of advancing his ministerial training.

---

[6] Chapter Thirteen has more to say on this subject.

Carl had known that the good people in Auroraville were in need and now he knew that his good friend in Milwaukee had a desire. He sought to harmonize these two dynamics and enable mutual satisfaction by making some suggestions on both sides. Something rather wonderful came out of his mediation.

A Lentz home meeting
***Ida Jordan** and son, front row center*
***Reinhold Sass**, back center - **Lydia and William Rayback**, far right*
***Lydia Sass and daughter LaVerne**, 4th from left*

When the time was right, Carl said to his friend, *"Reinhold, you and your family should move to Auroraville because the people of that church are ready to accept you as their pastor. Furthermore, I will be the mentor you seek!"*

Reinhold and Lydia had every reason to believe that Carl would keep this pledge of support. With confidence in both God and man, Reinhold Sass became the first official pastor for *The Church at Auroraville.*

Early in 1925, Reinhold, Lydia and their four-year-old daughter LaVerne moved out of the city and into the village. A ready-made, spirit-filled congregation warmly welcomed them to a spacious church building that offered roomy living quarters upstairs. It was time to celebrate the arrival of a parson to the parsonage and to the pulpit!

Pastor Sass succeeded in fanning the flame of Pentecost and *The Church in Auroraville* lent stability to the revival that God was giving throughout the area. This new leader had a vision to use the large facility in Auroraville for more than local purposes. The church agreed to host a convention in the fall after his arrival. It would be the first of many such gatherings that attracted people from diverse parts of the Midwest annually.[7]

The sign posted on the left of the "cheese factory" church is an announcement for the convention of October 22-30, 1925 that includes mention of Divine Healing services.
Reinhold Sass *is standing to the right at the entrance of the church.*

In the first couple years of operation, the "cheese factory" church was jubilant about the tremendous progress they were making, God working with them in miraculous

---

[7] You can read more about these annual conventions in Chapter Ten

ways. It was easy to believe that the good times would last forever. It was not to be, however. Less than two years after Pastor Sass arrived, a major crisis came out of nowhere and rocked their settled and secure world. The clear road ahead for the Sass family personally and *The Church at Auroraville* corporately was suddenly cluttered with debris coming straight from their own large storehouse of blessing.

Pastor Sass had taken his family away on a short winter trip back home to Milwaukee and while he was gone the old cheese factory building caught on fire and burned to the ground. It was unbelievable but true that, once again, most all earthly possessions belonging to the Sass family were gone in a flash. Except for their own precious family members and the few things they had taken with them to Milwaukee, the things belonging to this world had summarily gone up in flames.

The demise of the "cheese factory" church

Pastor Sass carried the dual load of making extremely difficult decisions for the family and for the church while also attempting to comfort all who mourned. Setting aside his own grief, he took heart in a heart-breaking situation and tended to the business at hand. Where were they to live and how were they to make a living? He and Lydia felt that they had no option but to return to familiar territory. In Milwaukee they could rebuild personally and also resolve a nagging problem they had left behind in the waking of moving to the village. The city still needed an apostolic church and it was time for them to do something about it once and for all. They were interrupted in reaching this goal only by accepting one last call to move away for outside ministry. An apostolic church in Antigo, Wisconsin needed a pastor and Reinhold took his family there for about a year to strengthen the church.

Once back in Milwaukee to stay, the Sass family succeeded in establishing a good congregation and concluded their lives right where they had begun as a newly married couple. Lydia became known as an excellent Friday night Bible teacher while Reinhold took care of the preaching in Sunday services. We pay tribute to this fervent, steadfast couple for their considerable contribution to the apostolic revival movement of the times.

Chapter Four

NEW CHURCH

What would become of the faithful in Auroraville after that fateful fire? Feelings of desolation swept over the congregation on the day they lost the building and weeping went on for years when remembering how it happened. It was a Sunday in the winter in the early afternoon when the fire broke out through the roof. The service had ended and people were leisurely eating packed lunches and enjoying each other's company. Some had smelled smoke in the building but no one could find the source. Abruptly, the calm and happy fellowship was broken and people were found, literally, out in the cold watching helplessly as their collective hopes and hard work disappeared before their very eyes. The shocking loss of the "cheese factory" church was a calamity for which there seemed to be no consolation.

Nevertheless, in true Auroraville fashion, the faithful would not let mourning keep them from the work at hand. This was not a time for the faint-hearted. They promptly found another place to rent for services and moved on. God's amazing grace carried them past despair and right into the next invigorating phase of their church history. It opened with a proposal that seemed too good to be true. Would they like to build on the charred ruins of their beloved church? Faith answered "yes" but facts forced other important considerations to the forefront. There were no funds in the church treasury for such a mammoth undertaking. How were they going to balance the facts with their faith?

The irrepressible people of *The Church at Auroraville* rose up to meet this challenge in a way that many would call risky business. Ignoring popular wisdom, they focused first on faith and second on the resources firmly in hand. The elders of the church agreed to sign for a bank loan, putting themselves personally in jeopardy. Recall, those were not prosperous times for farmers and they had no assurances, naturally speaking, that provision would be there for their homes and families, much less for the church. On the other hand, when Jesus said that life is more than meat and raiment, they knew He was right. This was a group of people who believed that the accompanying promise He gave was for them - *"so seek ye first the Kingdom of God and all these things shall be added unto you."*[8] With a mind to work and inspiration from the Word, they stepped out and purchased the lot, cleared the rubble and began building a new structure early in 1927.

If any one of the builders were alive today and could tell us something about the planning and construction stages of the new building, we would no doubt be astonished at how the initial vision came to fruition. The new Pentecostals in the village likely had no tried and true church blueprints to follow but yet they managed to successfully tailor-make a bit of a masterpiece for the times. From best recollections, a man from afar joined with builders in the church like William Rayback and Charles Dunham to make it happen. That man was Carl Ebert who had always maintained a personal interest in the welfare of the church. He brought his contracting expertise and tools to the village to see the church construction through to its conclusion. He is the one who probably coordinated the plans with the labor and spearheaded the inside finishing work.

The building was clearly designed with faith in mind. Sparing no cost, the builders included a parsonage when there was no preacher, a large fellowship hall when they

---

[8] Matthew 6:33

could only hope to continue hosting conferences and an indoor baptistery when they could not be sure the revival would continue. The latter feature would prove to accommodate everyone, providing year-round comfort and convenience. Most baptismal candidates would be locals but other apostolic believers and pastors were invited to drive in from any distance, especially during the cold winter months, to take advantage of the new indoor facility. Those with a way to get to Auroraville would no longer have to wait for a spring thaw to have their sins washed away.

The end result of faith, persistence, teamwork and ingenuity was a structure that rose up triumphantly out of the rubble, to give honor to the Lord right there in the middle of the village.

The Church at Auroraville
Nearing completion in late summer - 1927

When Pentecostal Assembly (*see the above church sign*) was sufficiently finished to open the doors to the public, Carl Ebert presented another gift to the people. He agreed to stay on and pastor the church. He brought his wife and youngest daughter with him when he assumed leadership, leaving his much-older daughters, young adults by then, in Eau Claire to work their jobs. All things considered, it was abundantly clear that the Great Provider had once again provided completely.

Carl, Martha and four-year-old Eunice must have felt privileged but overwhelmed to move into such a big "house" when they arrived in 1927. Eunice had grown into a healthy little girl since her dad prayed and believed for her healing some years before and she enjoyed the facility immensely. The pastor's living quarters in the rear of the first floor were generous and the entire interior was beautifully finished. A unique feature of this building created a favorite memory for young Eunice. The church was built over a running spring! While people in the village had to pump their water from outside wells, the

Ebert family could get a bucket of fresh, clean water from inside, any time of the day or night, any time of the year. Young Eunice felt like they had fallen straight into the lap of village luxury!

While the pastor's daughter was enjoying the handy flow of natural water, the parishioners were coming inside to be refreshed by another kind of water. That is, Jesus said that all those who believe on Him would have rivers of *living water* flowing from within to quench their spiritual thirst.[9] All indications are that a bountiful supply of this other kind of water was available as well inside the church.

Carl and Martha Ebert
Standing at the church entrance

With a new and spacious church now open for God's business and a qualified pastor on location to give regular spiritual guidance, the faithful members thought for sure that nothing would impede their progress going into the future. To their great surprise, something did come along to stop them dead in their tracks for much longer than anyone could have imagined.

This time, the culprit was a natural disaster of gigantic proportions. The worst winter in decades hammered the Midwest with more snow, ice, wind and bone-chilling temperatures than even Wisconsin winter warriors could handle. Roads were impassable; people sought shelter

---

[9] John 7:37-8

inside their homes for weeks on end just to be safe. The automobiles of the day were not built to withstand extreme outdoor conditions and neither were the people. Should a car start up in the bitter cold, the blustery blasts along open country roads were enough to make both driver and passengers think twice about going out again. The fear of sudden engine failure and the possibility of freezing to death were reasons enough to cancel all but the most urgent trips. Any journey had to be very short if it was to be sweet.

For most people in the church, no journey was short because they lived far from one another and far from the church. Isolated in the country, these people went into survival mode. They had to think as much about the farm animals as themselves. Every day brought a balancing act between protecting and sustaining the animals, equipment and buildings outside and keeping themselves safe and warm inside. Area residents endured an intense, all-consuming and exhausting daily routine throughout a very, very long winter.

Winter at the Millpond
The new church is the large white building to the left of center.

Gathering for worship and giving as always were out of the question. The church went into neutral but the mortgage still had to be paid. The church elders scrambled to keep ahead of the bank and Pastor Ebert watched helplessly as his personal finances dwindle away. The time came when he knew it was no longer feasible to stay on with the church. Of all the losses sustained in this round of reverses for the church, none was probably more keenly felt than the loss of their beloved pastor.

Thankfully, the building held up well through the winter and welcomed the weary congregation in the spring with brand new hope. The people had work to do for the Lord of the Harvest and believed He would provide other capable pastors to guide their work in the fields.

As for Pastor Ebert, he returned to Eau Claire to build yet another house or two. This was the routine of his life, continuously building, in one way or another, with a hammer and saw in one hand and a Bible in the other hand. At times, he pastored churches; at other times, he temporarily filled the pulpits of churches in need of evangelistic services or going through transitions between pastors. Regularly, he built houses to support his family and his ministry. At all times, he kept his pledge to preach, until, finally, that voice and those hands were stilled at age ninety.

Carl Frederick Ebert
A natural and spiritual builder

Chapter Five

THE MESSAGE SPREADS

The Church at Auroraville began to send out evangelistic teams as soon as the need was evident. Witnesses and workers went into cities like Antigo, Clintonville and Medford where churches were started with their assistance. Members of other growing communities were also obeying the command of the Lord, *"Go ye into all the world, and preach the gospel to every creature."*[10] Team members were motivated by a common purpose and became extremely effective evangelists willing to invest vast amounts of time and energy to reach souls.

Lay people came together out of their own initiatives to work for God who, in turn, was calling preachers and teachers to bring order in the church and feed the flocks. It was a time of renewal and organization, the Holy Ghost working through dedicated and enthusiastic people.

Believers from Eau Claire would travel many miles, west to the larger church in St. Paul and east to the smaller churches in Wisconsin, to evangelize and encourage one another. One report mentions a trip to far away Minot, North Dakota.[11] Zealous believers of all ages took musical instruments like trombones, saxophones, clarinets, violins and excellent singing voices out and about to enhance the preaching of the Gospel at every opportunity. Forgetting about time and long trips back to their own homes, these fervent ones would travel almost any distance to be in just one more meeting where like-minded people gathered to worship and learn from the Word.

---

[10] Mark 16:15
[11] Recollection – Ferinda Ebert Jordan

The photo below was taken during an evangelistic trip to Antigo. The names and faces are familiar with the exception of the woman wearing the hat. Pastor James Booker (West Bend, Wisconsin) believes this woman is his great grandmother who was a well-known speaker in Minnesota and Wisconsin at that time. She also served as a missionary to China and was said to be a spirited speaker with a great sense of humor.

Reinhold Sass, left
Lentz sisters, Esther, *seated on rail, and* ***Alice,*** *standing right*
Martha, Carl and Eunice Ebert, *middle*

Another city of significance in our continuing saga of the spread of Pentecost in central Wisconsin is Medford, located about one hundred and fifty miles northwest of Auroraville. Back in the 1920s, such a distance was a long way to go on mostly unpaved roads, for any reason. The ardor that characterized *The Church at Auroraville* found reason enough to make that particular long journey many, many times. At the outset, however, a man from Eau Claire named George Harris had to gain a spiritual foothold in this town.

George had an incredible conversion and, out of a thankful heart, testified effectively about it and was an uplifting presence everywhere that he went. Through Carl Ebert, George heard about the ministry of the Oelke family in Green Lake. The two men supported activities there in the early days of the revival and also when the church was finally and firmly established in Auroraville.

To ease the trip between Eau Claire and Auroraville, George would stop and spend the night with one or other of his two nieces in Medford. All he needed was an inquiry about the purpose of these repeated trips and George could tell them quite naturally that the power of Pentecost was available also for Medford! They were the first in the city to be converted, forming the core of yet another new church in north central Wisconsin.

The regular trips to Auroraville via Medford led to a wonderful working relationship between these two points of Pentecost. The new converts utilized the indoor baptistery in the village and the two groups supported each other through shared ministries and fellowship. When the Medford group began to outgrow the house meetings near the end of 1927, an earnest search for a meeting hall ended with the rental of a vacant store building. At that point, George Harris left his job in Eau Claire and moved to Medford where he assumed leadership of the flourishing new work of his own making.

Now, about that abandoned store building, we can surely say that God was in its selection for a church. A "GR" immigrant family living just down the street took note and became regular visitors to the services. This family had emigrated from the Volga region in Russia in 1906, looking for a better way of life in America. Now, some twenty years later, they would discover just how good life could really become. The gripping story of God's work in this family is featured later in this narrative.

Considering the outreach activities of the Auroraville church, it is natural and fitting to highlight an evangelistic team that surfaced in the late '20s and early '30s to be mightily used of God. This team is noteworthy for a number of reasons. For one, it was a traveling family group engaging in full-time ministry. For another, this group offered a strong healing ministry to the people.

By way of introduction to the larger story about this evangelistic group, it is interesting to note that the leader was a woman named Annabelle Harrington. She was the widowed mother of six children and would be fondly called Mother Harrington by all who knew and loved her. Her diary, kept in an address book, tells of one visit after another to remote areas in Wisconsin. Those who heard of her fervent and effectual prayers would write post cards requesting that she visit to pray for the sick and dying.

Annabelle was a dedicated and versatile servant of the Lord until a sudden stroke took her at age sixty-four. At her funeral in Oshkosh, the facility overflowed with those who came to pay their respects. A second service at the village cemetery afforded old associates a chance to say a fond farewell. As that graveside service concluded, a group approached the bereaved family members and a fellow among them burst into tears, saying,

> *"Who will lead us in prayer now that*
> *Mother Harrington is gone?"*

Chapter Six

HARRINGTON-HARDT HARMONY

In 1924, a young girl went to the altar and gave her heart to Jesus in the "cheese factory" church. Her mother wisely instructed her about the consequences of that decision as they hiked back home across the frozen millpond. This woman was Annabelle Harrington, who was already familiar with the Pentecostal message and the life style change that it would bring into the family. She was not yet ready to make her own commitment but felt a great sense of responsibility to guide her tenderhearted daughter. The young girl listened carefully to her mother's words and, being very sure of what she was doing, Sadie Alice Harrington came into the church at age ten and never looked back.

Sadie at age 15

As the spiritual drama of her life unfolded, she served wholeheartedly and effectively, first as an evangelist and later as an ordained minister in the U.P.C.I., fulfilling the roles of pastor's wife and area guest preacher. She lived out her Christian life circumspectly for sixty-eight years after this very early conversion set her on the pathway leading to eternal life.

Lee Harrington, the next oldest brother to Sadie, recorded a personal message for his family that gives a brief account of his introduction to Pentecost. It casts considerable light on the way things happened during this amazing time of pervasive revival, not only in Auroraville but also throughout America.

"I was about twelve years old when, one sunny day, I decided to take a walk into town and see what was happening and maybe find some of my friends. The Harrington farm was about a mile from the village center. I was quite a ways from the main road when I began to see a lot of traffic, as if it were the Fourth of July. I wondered what was going on. Along came a neighbor.

'Lee!' he said, 'You got to get down there. They are dunking folks in the millpond.' 'Doing what?' I asked. 'Baptizing! Get on down there and see for yourself!'

I never heard of baptizing so I went on down to see for myself. The banks of the millpond just below the dam were full of people watching just like me and another line of folks was standing by the water. Then, a fellow in the water would invite one in the line to come to him. He would raise his hands to heaven and pray a bit, then, dunk the person in the pond. There was considerable praying and shouting and then another person would get dunked or baptized! I had no idea what was going on down there."

This firsthand account confirms that residents from miles around Auroraville learned about Pentecost whether they wanted to or not! Some, like Lee, just happened by baptisms in progress; some came to check out reports they had heard of similar public spectacles; others came with open hearts and sincere questions and found themselves later lining up down by the river side.

Watching from his perch above the old millpond, Lee had no idea what was in store for his entire family. After Sadie came into Pentecost, Annabelle finally welcomed her own new beginning and Sadie's older siblings followed in her footsteps. The family collectively caught a vision of how to share the goodness of the Lord and they did it generously. As for that sunny summer day of first impressions, Lee could hardly imagine himself in line with the others being baptized, much less traveling with his family in evangelistic work.

Evangelist Howard Harrington

Howard, an even older brother to Sadie, developed a wonderful way of explaining the Scriptures to family and friends. People would stop by the Harrington farm for coffee and cake but their real hunger was for the Word of the Lord. Howard fed them well. They also came to sing the songs of Pentecost with Sadie playing the guitar. Sadie led them well. Mini- church services were an ongoing event in the family living room, most any time of the week and any time of the day. Howard began to exercise a healing ministry; the people would enter the house sick and depart from the house well. He was always quick to remind the ones experiencing miraculous healings that Jesus, not Howard Harrington, was the Healer of all diseases.

Spiritual growth in the members of the Harrington family was swift as they studied, prayed and poured themselves out in both home and church meetings. Doors to outside ministry began to open wide. Those who were experiencing Pentecost wanted their family and friends in other villages to hear the message. Invitations for home Bible studies in various locations began to mount. Soon,

Howard, the would-be farmer, was spending more time preaching and praying for the sick than working on the farm. A dynamic family evangelistic team had come of age and Mother Annabelle Harrington left Auroraville in the fall of 1928 with four of her grown children to launch a full-time evangelistic ministry. Their lives and times could fill a book all its own.

Young Sadie led the music side of ministry and she could bring people to their feet even at the age of fourteen. The family went from one revival service to another, widening their reach until meetings planned for two weeks in River Falls, Wisconsin in 1930 turned into a two-year revival. Howard became the first pastor of the people they won in that city and he stayed on even after the rest of the family made their way back home to a more settled life.

The Church at Auroraville heartily welcomed Mother Harrington and her family back in the village because the needs of the church were many. In depression times, keeping one step ahead of the bank in mortgage payments was not an easy task. Annabelle helped to manage the church finances, joining Fred Schmid, the church bookkeeper, more than once to negotiate contract revisions with the bank. Miraculously, this financial team succeeded in forestalling foreclosure until the mortgage was completely paid off. Mother Harrington was a prayer warrior who also led services and inspired the saints, especially when the church found itself without a pastor.

While still a traveling team, we know that the Harringtons went northwest more than once to help strengthen the budding group in Medford, Wisconsin. Gottlieb Hardt was the "GR" man living with his family down the street when the store building was transformed into a church. A surprise turn of events would change their status overnight from regular visitors to proper Pentecostals!

Mother Harrington came to minister in Medford with her daughter and a missionary from China, making quite a spiritual impression on the young son of Gottlieb, Samuel Hardt. When Evangelist Howard Harrington came later, accompanied by his sister Sadie and Billy Page, the converted Lentz farmhand, Samuel was more than impressed. He was moved to unexpected action.

On a Sunday he came forward to be baptized in water and was filled with the Holy Ghost that very same day. On Monday, Billy Page and another brother went to an afternoon prayer meeting at the Hardt home and Samuel's mother received the Holy Ghost. That evening, Gottlieb excused himself from the dinner table to go pray alone at his bedside. The visiting brethren and other family members decided to leave their food also and gathered in prayer around this seeking soul. The glory of the LORD came into the room and the head of the Hardt household was also filled with the Holy Ghost!

Medford Church in 1928
Samuel Hardt, *2nd from the right*
Gottlieb Hardt and his wife, *1st and 2nd from the left*

This was the astounding beginning for a family whose believing members in succeeding generations are scattered all across America, including an ambassador who served the Vatican and had opportunity to explain Pentecostal views and practices to the Pope, the head of the Roman Catholic Church.

Samuel recounts that he was quite taken with the music ministry of young Sadie Harrington on both occasions that her family visited Medford. He and she did not interact, however, in any personal way until much later. Samuel was just fourteen years old when he surrendered to God and began to follow his call to the ministry. Sadie traveled into her late teens, helping the family with many evangelistic campaigns.

By age fifteen, Samuel was known as the "boy preacher" because of his blazing deliveries in the pulpit at a young age. His reputation spread throughout the Midwest and he was an assistant pastor in Duluth, Minnesota by age seventeen. When Howard Harrington invited him to move to River Falls to fill in for his temporary but necessary absence from the church, Samuel was able to accept and had some wonderful surprises in store.

Sadie was in River Falls, engaged in the revival campaign that was well into its second year when Samuel arrived. The two young people found time and opportunity to discover the many life experiences that they had in common. They were the same age, now both seventeen; they were the first in their families to be converted; each had led their entire families into the church; each had developed powerful ministries while still in their teens.

A firm friendship ensued that endured even through times of separation. Howard Harrington came back to pastor in River Falls and Samuel Hardt left to resume his evangelistic ministry. About the time the Harrington family felt to leave River Falls for home, news reached them of an outbreak of revival in Rush River, Wisconsin. Evangelist Samuel Hardt was holding dynamic meetings there and Mother Harrington stopped by to see if the evangelist could use some help from an evangelistic team. Of course he could! They stayed on for several months as the Rush River revival continued to flourish right along with the friendship between Sadie and Samuel.

At the ripe young age of twenty, these two young evangelists realized that a very good friendship had turned into a wonderful romance and it was time to marry. On May 15, 1934, they said their vows at the altar of the Auroraville church with Pastor W. A. Mulford officiating. Deeply devoted to one another and to their Lord, this couple began a loving partnership that ended only when Sadie preceded Samuel in death at age seventy-eight. As this book is being published, he is living out his last years comfortably, anticipating a glad and glorious reunion with his wife and his Lord!

In 1938, **Samuel and Sadie Hardt** *at age 24*

Three generations
Mother Annabelle Harrington, *on the right*
Sadie Harrington Hardt *(daughter)*, *on the left*
Jon Hardt *(firstborn to Sadie)*, *on her lap*

Chapter Seven

FAITHFUL UNTO DEATH

One of the notable pastors of *The Church at Auroraville* deserves a place in this chronicle because of what he was unable to do, as much as for what he was able to do. Let's begin by citing a small contribution he made to someone else's life journey. Pastor Joseph Sarges[12] was serving the church in Auroraville in the early 1930s as Fred and Pauline Lentz continued their strident witnessing for the Lord. The Lentz daughters, Alice and Esther, had grown into young women willing to offer their musical talents regularly to their home church and to any other gathering in which they were needed.

In 1931, Andrew D. Urshan was preaching for Pastor Sarges in Auroraville when his youngest brother by twenty-two years, Evangelist Benjamin Urshan, was simultaneously preaching in Eau Claire. Andrew sent a letter strongly urging Ben to make his way to the village after he was finished in the city. The purported purposes were a preaching engagement for the young people in the church *and* an opportunity to meet a talented and attractive young lady named Alice.

Suspecting what was the prime reason for his brother's nudge toward Auroraville, Ben did try to get to the village by public transportation. The nearest connection was Oshkosh and that was not close enough, so he closed the meeting in Eau Claire and went straight home to Chicago instead, missing his first chance to meet Alice. When Andrew joined Benjamin later, with a photo of that young lady, Ben realized that he had made a very big mistake.

---

[12] alternately spelled *Sargis*

Pastor Sarges was the next one to get a letter, this one from Evangelist Ben Urshan, entreating the pastor to allow him to hold a meeting for the church young people! Pastor Sarges accommodated him and Ben finally met Alice. It was love at first sight for both of them.[13]

Midway Tabernacle in St. Paul, Minnesota invited Ben to be their pastor soon after he met Alice. In 1932, they were married and ministered together there for over two years, going on to pastor in Duluth, Minnesota for twenty-five years. In 1960, they left for Ben's homeland of Iran as missionaries. Unfortunately, this mission was cut short after eighteen months because of visa restrictions. Ben and Alice finished out their many fruitful years of ministry in America by assuming pastorates in Clintonville, Wisconsin for almost five years and Albuquerque, New Mexico for almost seventeen years. They left a fine legacy to all family, friends and church members who were blessed to know them.

The second Lentz daughter, Esther, married Wendell Haskins and both have been zealous participants, along with their two daughters, for many years in various Wisconsin churches, including Oshkosh, Clintonville and Fond du Lac. In their prime, with Esther at the piano and Wendell leading the singing, many a church service got off to a rousing start. Esther actually initially inspired the writing of these narratives.

Pastor Sarges and his family were still at the helm of *The Church at Auroraville* in the perilous winter of 1932-33 when exceptionally cold weather teamed up with an influenza epidemic and waged war on the general population. Some won in the battle and others did not. Every member of Pastor Sarges' family recovered fully by the time the inhospitable winter was over, except for one.

---

[13] *Survivor, The Life Story of Benjamin Urshan*

It was Pastor Sarges himself who finally succumbed after months of struggle to survive.

"He would get better, then worse.
Then, one day he was no longer with us."[14]

At age 37, in the summer of 1933, Joseph Sarges died in the line of duty. After the burial, his wife wanted to go back to her home state where she and her three children could find solace and support from her own family. The church collected enough money to secure a burial plot and managed to do the same to purchase train tickets for her and the children.

Esther Haskins recalls that, on a dreary day, several saints from the church took a forlorn mother and three bewildered children to the Berlin train station. It was a fond farewell to the living but a faltering farewell to the dead. Joseph remained behind, at rest in the Auroraville cemetery in a grave unmarked due to lack of funds. His gravesite would

The Joseph Sarges Family

remain for some years in anonymity, in a locale that circumstances determined would be inconvenient and financially inaccessible to immediate family members.

---

[14] Recollection - Esther Haskins

This very sad and unfortunate situation exemplifies the kind of price that some preachers and their families had to pay to advance the Gospel during the early period of Pentecostal renewal.

It is wonderful to report that, as God would have it, appropriate remembrance of Pastor Joseph Sarges did eventually come along in a unique and noble way. Lee Harrington, the one who stood overlooking a baptismal service on the banks of the old millpond many years before, came back on the scene and did a very good deed. Lee had gone into the military and when he returned to Wisconsin, he learned of the preacher who died and was buried with less recognition on this earth than he deserved. Lee made it his mission to find the burial site of Joseph Sarges and began yearly spring pilgrimages with flowers to respectfully mark it.

Years later, James Harrington heard the touching story and was motivated to further his father's mission after some unexpected recognition came his way. James was also a pastor, ordained in the Methodist Church. While serving in Janesville, Wisconsin, he was volunteering at a nursing home, stopping by to visit and conduct services for the elderly. These grateful residents decided to express their appreciation in an uncommon way. They put together a cash offering and proudly presented it to a very surprised and pleased preacher. Jim was so moved by this generosity that he mused for a long while about how to use the money. When he reached a decision, implementation followed quickly. Adding funds of his own to the gift already in hand from the nursing home residents, the Reverend James Harrington was able to buy a very nice gravestone for the Reverend Joseph Sarges!

"I have fought a good fight;
I have finished my course;
I have kept the faith:

Henceforth, there is laid up for me
a crown of righteousness,
which the Lord, the righteous judge,
shall give me at that day: and not to me only,
but unto all them also that love his appearing."

II Timothy 4:7-8

Auroraville church gathering in the early 1940's

1st row, left to right
Carl Trittin, Gottlieb Hardt
2nd row, left to right
The Smiths, Reinhold Sass, Evangelist Marsh, Lydia Hardt
3rd row, left to right
The Benjamin Urshans, Lydia Sass, Harry Daley *and wife,*
Clyde Daley *and wife*
4th row
Joseph Elstad*, right of* **Harry Daley**
Jim Peterson*, just behind Joseph*
Marie Peterson*, behind and to the left of Harry*

The Church at Auroraville

Chapter Eight

BRIGHT BEAMS

Philip P. Bliss wrote a hymn that *The Church at Auroraville* must have sung often because they lived out its message. The melody and lyrics are simple but powerful, the kind to spur most any caring heart into action.

> *Brightly beams our Father's mercy,*
> *from His lighthouse evermore.*
> *But, to us, He gives the keeping,*
> *of the lights along the shore.*
>
> *Let the lower lights be burning!*
> *Send a gleam across the wave.*
> *Some poor fainting, struggling seaman,*
> *you many rescue, you may save.*

The Church at Auroraville made it their business to keep lower lights burning year after year, always ready to rescue one more person struggling on the sea of life. Marie Brant Peterson was a young lady looking to be found from a long way off. The Light from the Lighthouse sent strong signals out to her as far as God's own Word could reach but it took others with the lower lights along the shore to complete the rescue operation. *The Church at Auroraville* was on duty when Marie needed them most. Her story is nicely told in two distinct scenes.

Scene I: Pre-Pentecost
Marie was born into a large farm family in Polar, Wisconsin, north and remote from any sizeable town. She was one of the younger family members who found a special friend for the lonely days on the farm. Someone

had brought a Bible into the house and it became her constant companion. At first, she enjoyed reading just for pleasure but, somewhere along the line, she found herself becoming a self-taught Bible scholar. She started comparing scriptures and searching for deeper meanings beneath the surface history and dramatic events.

Marie Brant Peterson

Marie had an older married sister living south in Embarrass, Wisconsin, just north of Clintonville, who needed help with her growing family. Marie agreed to go down and lend a helping hand for a while. This supposed short pause in life took her down a road that would never turn back to Polar. It was all Jim's fault. He was a local cavalier lad who was smitten by the sight of Marie and thanked his lucky stars that it was a mutual attraction. In due season they got married and began farming their own land, a natural thing to do since both had been reared on a farm.

There was one major thing that this couple did not have in common, however. Thankfully, it never became problematic for either of them. Jim did not share Marie's interest in the Bible but was not put off in any obvious way by her intensity to learn from it. She continued her studies in peace after they married and her spiritual hunger remained insatiable. Her family and friends became accustomed to hearing one particular question from Marie time and time again. "Why is it", she would ask, "that the churches I find to attend now are so different from those that I read about in the book of Acts?" No one had an answer for her. Those who knew her well figured that she would be asking that same question until some day, somewhere, some church would be found within reach to be similar to the early church.

It was Jim's father, ironically, who was instrumental in bringing Marie's long quest to an end. It happened quite by "chance". He was taking care of his own business in town one day when he overheard some fellows talking about a church in Auroraville that required its members to be baptized by immersion, that is, "dunked" in a creek. The conversation did not catch his full attention until he heard someone add that these folks not only got "dunked" but they got "drunk" and, furthermore, spoke in "other tongues" just like described in the Bible.

At that point, he began to ask the questions he thought Marie would ask, because he knew this was a subject dear to her heart. Could this church possibly be the one his daughter-in-law was desperately hoping to find? He got directions for the seventy-mile trip to the village and made plans to get over to Jim's farm as soon as possible to share this extraordinary news.

When Marie finally heard the story about her father-in-law's encounter in town, she was ecstatic. He offered to take her to Auroraville if she thought the trip would not become a wild goose chase. Without hesitation, Marie said, "I want to go!" It was settled. The two of them would travel as soon as they could possibly get away.

News of the plan hatched by his wife and his father brought an interesting reaction from Jim. He wanted to join the party but only because he was curious. His idea of a good party was something quite earthy, the kind he was used to organizing in the community that had nothing to do with religion or church. He asked if he might go along for the ride and, in the end, Jim's dad drove south with Marie, Jim and their two children in the dependable family

Studebaker to Auroraville. It was the late 1920s and the long trip over gravel roads at forty miles per hour made for a rather rigorous ride. There is no doubt that the incentive for this trip flew in the face of natural reason but Marie was willing to do whatever it took to possibly bring a life-long search for a church to an end.

The group from the village of Embarrass arrived late for that first meeting and walked into a stirring service already in progress. The proceedings went on much longer than expected but the family agreed to stay with Marie until the very end, listening carefully to the sermons and keenly observing how these very enthusiastic twentieth-century Christians worshipped. Marie noticed immediately that this church was much like one she had longed to find. She felt instantly and totally at home.

On the return journey in the dark of night, Jim's dad suspected the answer to his question but asked anyway. "Do you think you've finally found your dream church?" he queried. Her speedy response left no doubt. She soundly declared, "I want to go back and be baptized as soon as I can!" She did go back, again and again and again and never alone. No rugged ride was too much to bear in view of the abundance of blessing at the end of the journey. Her son, John Peterson, who was probably four years old at the time, recalls those trips, saying that sometimes the services were so intense that his folks forgot about the time. It would be one or two o'clock in the morning in Auroraville before they were ready to begin the long drive back home to the farm work awaiting them in Embarrass. They handled those glorious late night "parties" by sleeping awhile on the hard floor of the sanctuary to gain strength before piling into the old Studebaker and heading home in time for sunrise milking and feeding of the animals.

As already mentioned, Marie always had company going to Auroraville. Her husband faithfully escorted her back and forth. The change in her was remarkable and all the family, particularly Jim, took note of the improvements. His initial tolerance gave way to genuine support for Marie's new demeanor. She exhibited the fruits of the Spirit so convincingly that Jim started wanting similar changes in his own life. In the end, he decided that the Pentecostal way was a worthy way for himself as well as his wife and he began to seek his own salvation.

In fact, when he became desperate, he began to spend all his spare time in between farm chores in prayer. He would go to a favorite place, the hall between the silo and the barn, to seek for the infilling of the Holy Spirit. One glorious day, in divine response to his diligence, he began to speak in tongues as the Spirit gave him the utterance.[15]

Scene II: Post-Pentecost
The Petersons walked together into the second season of Marie's life where a whole new way of living was waiting for them. How would they spend their spare time, in the midst of the hard work of farming, now that they were fully committed Christians? Naturally, they would start holding services in their home! It was the trend of the times on the way to establishing a church. Jim and Marie became exceptional witnesses who enjoyed the support of seasoned ministers like Carl Trittin, Carl Ebert, Reinhold Sass and young evangelist Samuel Hardt. These men came in to help reap and retain the harvest of souls and were given generous support by the group of believers in and around Embarrass in return for their sound preaching and teaching. The home meetings eventually produced a cohesive core of believers who concluded that the best location for their ballooning church would be in the nearby city of Clintonville. That church has stood the test of time

---

[15] Acts 2:4

and is now under the banner of the U.P.C.I. with members down to the fourth generation since Auroraville promoting Pentecost faithfully in that part of Wisconsin.

For a time, Reinhold Sass, who was settled in Milwaukee to pastor, traveled regularly up to Clintonville to lead the new church. Inevitably, the time came when practicality had its way and Reinhold arranged a meeting with Jim to discuss the future of the church. A very interesting conversation ensued that got right to the point.

With regrets, Reinhold explained that it was no longer possible for him to pastor the Clintonville group from afar. Jim followed this disclosure with a key question. "What will we do for a pastor?" Reinhold's reply was decisive. "YOU will become the pastor." This directive brought a protest. "I'm a farmer," said Jim. "How can I be a pastor?" Without skipping a beat, Reinhold Sass replied, "You'll have to pray a lot." Conversation over.

Jim and Marie Peterson

Jim Peterson took on the dual roles of pastor and farmer. He and Marie kept their lower lights burning during all the remaining years of their lives. The Light from the Lighthouse had shone brightly on them and they wanted to pass it along to others.

"Let your light so shine before men, that they may see your good works and glorify your Father which is in heaven."
Matthew 5:16

Chapter Nine

FOND MEMORIES

The fine members of *The Church at Auroraville* and their equally fine pastors conscientiously met the church mortgage payments until the debt was retired. It was understood that pastors had to live lean on what the congregation could provide or subsidize the giving of the church with personal funds. Consequently, many a fine man of God came but did not necessarily pastor the church for a long period of time. Also, there was a lot of fluidity in the ministry in those times and short-term pastorates were very common. Whether a ministering family stayed a few months, a year or even longer, the congregation in Auroraville was always good to supply fresh garden fruits and vegetables, farm meat, eggs and, probably, a lot of home-baked goods thrown in for good measure. A few dollars of cash would be added each week to these bountiful donations in support of the ministry.

One couple comes to mind that considered their time of service in Auroraville to be a genuine privilege. Samuel and Sadie Hardt revived fond memories when they returned to the village in 1937 to pastor the church. Sadie had surrendered her life to God in the old building and they had said their wedding vows together in the new building. Now, the time had come to give back. With their three-year-old son in tow, they returned to familiar surroundings to be a blessing.

The church offered three dollars a week in addition to free residence in the pastor's quarters in the rear of the spacious building. The young family felt that the financial incentive was sufficient and agreed to take on the pastoral challenge. The weekly cash offerings covered a car payment and other basic personal expenses; food offerings from the church people provided healthy and delicious fare. They stayed on duty for an entire year, adding to their collection of fond memories.

Samuel relates that funds provided for him as a pastor in Auroraville were actually better than some he had received as an evangelist on the road. A church in Racine, Wisconsin, for example, has records showing that Evangelist Samuel Hardt was rewarded for one week of ministry with just thirty-five cents! While it might be difficult to determine now exactly how much purchasing power thirty-five cents had then, it is probably safe to say that it was not enough to start a savings account or even stay out of debt!

Sometimes a traveling preacher had difficulty collecting enough money for bus or train fare to the next town for the next meeting. Hitchhiking was a common way for the young and single men to solve that problem. When the money was not in the hand, the thumb knew how to travel without it. It is said that Samuel Hardt became quite an expert traveler using this economical, although unsafe, way to get around. No reports of trouble during those traveling days have surfaced so we have to believe that divine protection went with him on every journey.

It is admirable, to say the least, that finances never dictated or dissuaded the dedication of circuit preachers and resident pastors in those early days of Pentecost in America. Gifted and anointed men and women were energized by the exceptional things God was doing through their ministries. We may never know the full extent of the volunteer service that they rendered but we know that it was common to give until there was just no more to give. Preachers were answering the call to become fishers of men and fishing was mighty good in many places, including by the old millpond.

Chapter Ten

CONFERENCES AND FELLOWSHIP

The first Wisconsin Apostolic Pentecostal Ministers Conference was held in *The Church at Auroraville* in 1925. A successful opener called for a repeat performance and soon the village church was hosting annual conventions.

Eventually lay people were invited to join in and it became the "in" thing for Pentecostals from as far away as Indianapolis and St. Louis to participate. Overnight facilities were limited but people tackled that problem by bringing their own house trailers or tents for camping on the grounds. Others were heartily invited into the homes of the Auroraville saints who always seemed to have room for just one more. Whole families would come and older children brought their fishing poles. The stories of fishing off the millpond bridge would get bigger and bigger, particularly concerning the ones that got away!

Ministers sought the counsel of elders to resolve problems; lay people and ministers were strengthened in the doctrines of the church through Bible teaching and refreshed through dynamic preaching and lively worship in the presence of the Lord. The gatherings served to consolidate apostolic doctrine and practice in the Midwest.

In 1937, Reverend Stuart G. Norris opened Apostolic Bible Institute (A.B.I.) in St. Paul, Minnesota. He began with a one-year program of study that expanded to a three-year program that has trained thousands of apostolics from all over America over many decades. In the early days, he and members of his school and church staff supported the ongoing revival in Wisconsin with encouragement and sound systematic teaching.

Preachers attending a Ministers' Conference - circa 1940

Identifiers are on the next page.

*** Unidentified Persons

Front Row, left to right:
(1) ***
(2) **George Bye**, *St. Paul, MN*
(3) **Wallace McKeehan**, *A.B.I.*
(4) **Clyde Daley**, *Platteville, WI*
(5) **Carl Trittin**, *Appleton, WI*
(6) **Gottlieb Hardt**, *Medford, WI*
(7) **James Marsh**, *Evangelist*
(8) **Harry Rubin**, *Milwaukee, WI*

Middle Row, left to right:
(1) **Henry Gerue**, *Withee, WI*
(2) **Jim Peterson**, *Clintonville, WI*
(3) ***
(4) **Dorothy Gilmore**, *Evangelist*
(5) **Reinhold Sass**, *Milwaukee, WI*
(6) ***
(7) **Fred Scott**, *A.B.I.*

Back Row, left to right:
(1) ***
(2 **Benjamin Urshan**, *Duluth, MN*
(3) **Howard Harrington**, *Evangelist*
(4) ***
(5) **Joseph Brooks**, *Beloit, WI*
(6) ***
(7) **Stuart G. Norris**, *St. Paul, MN*
(8) **Milton Buller**, *A.B.I.*
(9) **George Dainty**, *Spencer, IA*
(10) **M.S. Wasko**, *River Falls, WI*
(11) **Richard Davis**, *Auroraville, WI*

Auroraville Church gathering in the late 1930s

Joseph Elstad, 2nd left - **Pauline and Fred Lentz**, 3rd and 4th left
Ellen Elstad, 5th left - **Emily and Charles Dunham**, 1st and 2nd right

Chapter Eleven

OPEN-ENDED CLOSURE

The Church at Auroraville, true to its rationale for being, was always a regional assembly. The people had to travel many a miserable mile on rugged roads even in mild weather, never mind throughout the winters, to gather together. Times had become tough in the 1930s for all levels of society. These factors make the history we are recounting all the more awe-inspiring. Nothing seemed to deter these tenacious believers. Then, along came World War Two and the face of America was changed forever.

right to left
Fred and Ida Schmid, 1st *and* 2nd
Esther and Wendell Haskins, 3rd *and* 4th
Fred and Pauline Lentz, 5th *and* 6th
left to right
Annabelle Harrington, 2nd
Emily Dunham, 6th

The war years (1941–1945) had a huge impact on this side of the Atlantic and Pacific Oceans even though not one shot was fired here. Young men were called away to serve "Uncle Sam" and women left home for the workplace. Farm folks became city folks and worked in defense industries. Gas, food and even clothes were rationed. The negative effect on *The Church at Auroraville* was enormous but they kept the doors open and even managed to host the annual conferences during the war.

In 1945, when the war was officially over, the damage to America's farmland was not physical but decidedly economic. The family farm was no longer the ideal and young men did not go back to pick up where they had left off when called to war. Neighbors sold out to other neighbors who thought they could succeed if only they owned more land, more equipment or more livestock.

By the middle of the '40s, it was clear to the Wisconsin ministerial leadership that the mother church in Auroraville had fulfilled its mission. It did not abandon the people nor did the people abandon it. Essentially, the times abandoned them both. Thankfully, apostolic Pentecostal churches had blossomed in surrounding towns, owing largely to the untiring efforts of those going out from Auroraville, so that alternative houses of worship were available to the people.

The closure of *The Church at Auroraville* comes with an interesting aside. The last official pastor was Richard Davis who had moved from Ohio in 1937 to attend A.B.I. in Minnesota. After the one year of study, he returned to Ohio but eventually settled in Wisconsin to serve in Auroraville and later Pentecostal Assembly in Eau Claire as pastor for sixteen years. Pastor Davis recalls that he had the unhappy task of signing the papers that finalized the sale of the church property. It was sold in 1946 without any fashion of fanfare.

Once the building in Auroraville closed its doors, the true church, the Body of Christ, went on with its business. In its heyday, when the natural and spiritual enterprises were one, *The Church at Auroraville* did not necessarily achieve notoriety by earthly measure. Now, almost a century later, it is obvious that its influence has been phenomenal by heavenly measure.

Thousands can trace their spiritual beginnings to the time when people in the pulpit and people in the pews of this extraordinary church would allow nothing short of war and winter to interfere with their pursuit of excellence in soul-winning. The closure of this church is open-ended in that the influence of those who came in to be saved and went out to witness goes on *ad infinitum.*

1941
Auroraville Main Street
In the distance, the white building to the left of the road is the church.

Chapter Twelve

UNTO ALL GENERATIONS

The Auroraville story is like a tapestry in the making. It is clearly a splendid piece of God's handiwork thus far. The weaving began with many kinds of threads, some of them still strong enough to be woven further and further into the enlarging fabric. Other threads weakened along the way and broke off but their strong ends have been tied securely to the back so that every contributing strand remains firmly in place. New threads are added in continuously, mixing their fresh and bright colors, hues and contemporary patterns with the seasoned, deeper tones and traditional patterns, enriching the weave.

It is impossible to identify the myriad of threads that fashion this elaborate tapestry. Many have become obscure in the density of the weaving. Should we try to trace the exposed threads from this generation backward, the exercise would go way beyond the scope of this book.

Instead, we have settled on displaying an abbreviated family tree, the branches of our hero and heroine, Carl and Rosa Ebert. It will substantiate a point already made. That is, in less than thirty years of active ministry, the impact of *The Church at Auroraville* on the apostolic Pentecostal movement, particularly the U.P.C.I., is very impressive.

The numbers appearing before the names indicate the generation, starting with Carl or Rosa as the first generation, going on as far as the sixth generation, along one family line. It must be noted that only the skeleton of a standard family tree is presented here because some descendants are unknown and, also, because brevity lends itself to our purpose.

1Carl Frederick (Martha) Ebert
  2Ferinda Ebert (Herbert) Jordan
    3Donald (Rosalee) Jordan
      4Jennifer, 4Steven, 4Sheila
    3Joanne (Tom, *deceased*) Lewis
      4Lori, 4Nancy, 4Shelley, 4Jeff, 4John
    3Lois (Roy,*deceased U.P.C.I. licensed minister*) Taylor (Buddy) Tamel
      4Michael, 4Ann
    3Nancy (William, *U.P.C.I. licensed minister*) Sciscoe
      4Julie (Dr. Jerry, *U.P.C.I. licensed minister*) Smucker
                          5Austin, 5 Jessica
      4Jane (Bill, *U.P.C.I. licensed minister*) Pellum
                          5Natalie, 5Brooke, 5Logan, 5Olivia
      4Jason, *U.P.C.I. licensed minister* (Kimberly) Sciscoe
                          5Julianna
  2Ardys Ebert (Walter) Moehlenpah
    3Jocelyn Moehlenpah Eastland
      4Elizabeth, 4Robert, 4Thomas
    3Donn, *U.P.C.I. licensed minister from 1963-76 (Joy)* Moehlenpah
      4Timothy   5Grace, 5Lauren, 5Robert
      4Carl Andrew   5Amanda, 5Alexi, 5Daniel
      4Lisa Valletta   5Alyssa, 5Maria, 5Sophia
      4Donn Philip   5Ashley, 5Aubrey, 5Christopher
      4Sarah Alexander   5David, 5Graeme, 5Anna
    3Dr. Arlo, *U.P.C.I. licensed minister* (Jane) Moehlenpah
      4Ed   5Jonathan, 5Krista, 5Kayla, 5Jaron
      4Glenda
      4Sam, *U.P.C.I. licensed minister*   5Joshlyn, 5Atalie
  2Eunice Ebert (Gordon - *deceased*) Buckli (Ray) Glenna
    3Jeanne, *deceased* (Patrick) Harmon
      4Amy   5Megan, 5Hailey
      4Michael   5Aiden
    3Jerilyn (David) Kiner
      4Kara   5Jacinta, 5Alexis
      4Jason   5Davida, 5Abigail, 5Gabrielle, 5Jada
      4Jeremy   5Dalyn, 5Weston
      4Krista   5Liberty
    3Barbara (Derrald, *U.P.C.I. licensed minister*) Hilderbrand
      4Bethany Hilderbrand
      4Brooke (Wes, *A.L.J.C. licensed minister*) Comer
                          5Isaiah, 5Emma, 5Joel, 5Eliza

1Rosa Ebert (Edward) Oelke
  2Reuben (Marjorie) Oelke
    3Robert (Carole, *granddaughter to Gottlieb Hardt*) Oelke
      4Kristin (John) Contino
        5Nicholas, 5Benjamin, 5Natalie
      4Dr. Kurt (Jan) Oelke
        5Gracyn, 5Keller
    3Donna (George) Miller
      4Michael (Debra) Miller
        5Derek (Sarah) Miller
          6Brianna
        5Mandi (Jon) Osborn
          6Caeden, 6Evan, 6Audrey, 6Kalista
        5Collin Miller
        5Nicole Miller
      4Greg (Kristell) Miller
        5Alyssa
        5Austin
        5Brooke
        5Ava
        5Benjamin
      4Marita (Stephen) Peters
        5Natalie, 5Emily, 5Zachary
    3Mary Leonardson (Pat) Geissler
      4Grady (Mary Jo) Leonardson
        5Aleksander, 5Grace
      4Margo (Matthew) Griffin
        5Madison
      4Eric (Janet) Leonardson
        5Laura, 5Lydia

  2Jimmy Oelke (adopted child who died very young

Carl Ebert and Rosa Ebert Oelke exerted a powerful spiritual influence within their extended families. The following family strands are some, but not all, that demonstrate this fact.

- Carl (through daughter Ferinda and granddaughter Nancy) has three great grandchildren and seven great, great grandchildren. ALL these are actively involved in U.P.C.I. churches and the extended family includes four licensed ministers serving presently in **Ohio.**

- Carl (through daughter Ardys and grandson Arlo) has three great grandchildren and six great, great grandchildren. ALL these are actively involved in U.P.C.I. churches and the extended family includes two licensed ministers serving presently in **California.**

- Carl (through daughter Eunice and granddaughter Barbara) has two great grandchildren and four great, great grandchildren. ALL these are actively involved in apostolic churches and the extended family includes a licensed U.P.C.I. minister serving presently in **Wisconsin** and a licensed A.L.J.C. minister serving presently in **Tennessee**.

- Rosa (through one son Reuben and all three grandchildren) has eight great grandchildren and twenty-two great, great grandchildren and five great, great, great grandchildren. ALL these are actively involved in nine different U.P.C.I. churches in either **Wisconsin** or **Minnesota**.

Chapter Thirteen

A FAR-REACHING THREAD

Our third and final story thread was deemed worthy to be told because it illuminates the worldwide influence of *The Church at Auroraville*. This thread stretches way beyond home territory and into some far reaches of the earth. The thread, a lone strand mercifully brought into the tapestry, has become interwoven with other more substantial threads, through marriage, as only the Master Weaver can do it. Valerie Demos will tell this concluding story because it is her own.

"Interest in our apostolic history drew me into this book project without a doubt. However, my personal attachment to the story firmly sealed the deal for me. It is a great honor to join in celebrating the lives of gospel groundbreakers because some have molded my life in significant and wonderful ways.

It was Samuel and Sadie Hardt who came along and introduced me to Pentecost. Well, actually, their daughter Sharon was the one who led the way. When her parents moved to Marshfield, Wisconsin to pastor an apostolic church, Sharon and I met and became best friends. Her knowledge of the Bible brought me face to face with my own ignorance; the invitations to attend her church brought me into the sweet and powerful presence of the Lord for the first time in my life; the love and kindness of her parents warmed me personally, their great skills in teaching and preaching brought conviction to my searching soul. In short, although I did not know it then, I became an Auroraville offspring because God sent the Hardt family to my city and into my life personally.

In my senior year of high school, I made a commitment to the Lord and obeyed the gospel. I purposely chose a college town where I could attend a recommended apostolic Pentecostal church while studying to become a high school math teacher. When I graduated from UW-Eau Claire, the spiritual highlight of my four years of student life was faithful membership in Pentecostal Assembly. I was abundantly blessed there but had yet to realize the historical connection between that church, the Marshfield church, Auroraville and my life. That understanding has finally come full circle through involvement in this book project.

I spent many life-changing hours in prayer at the altar in Pentecostal Assembly and accepted that God was calling me to the mission field. In due time, it was a very clear call to an unspecified country. In reflection, I realized that God had begun wooing me before I left home for college, especially through music. The lyrics and melody of one particular song moved me so often and so deeply that it is still etched in my memory, over fifty years later.

"Hear the Lord of Harvest sweetly calling,
Who will come and work for me today?
Who will bring to me the lost and dying?
Who will point them to the narrow way?

Speak, my Lord. Speak, my Lord.
Speak and I'll be quick to answer Thee.
Speak, my Lord. Speak, my Lord.
Speak and I will answer, Lord, send me."

In Eau Claire, the Lord did speak and I answered. I had no idea, however, when, where or how I would be sent.

While a college student, I spent a summer working in St. Paul, Minnesota where Alan Demos was raised under the ministry of an uncle and aunt, Stuart and Jessie Norris.

His family history is closely intertwined with the Andrew D. Urshan family through pastoral and friendship relationships. Alan and I met briefly that summer but it took a number of years for us to realize that our threads were meant to intertwine for a lifetime. When he felt to divulge his own dramatic call to the mission field, specifically to Greece, and learned of mine to anywhere and everywhere, we knew that our relationship was about more than personal pleasure and planning. He finished his studies at Butler University and immediately enrolled at A.B.I. to begin three years of study for the ministry, during which time we married.

Miraculously, God opened a door so we could enter and stay in the country of Greece as missionaries. Democracy was suddenly restored in the summer of 1975, just as we had finished our missionary deputation and wanted to move on location. We went with our four-year-old daughter Laura into a strange new world where there was not one apostolic believer. In fifteen years of ministry in Athens, we established the Crossroads International Christian Center visited by people from some eighty different nations. More importantly, people from forty different nations became truly apostolic believers!

Most of those converts have moved out from Athens and are living around the world, disseminating the apostolic message as preachers, teachers and faithful saints – in Great Britain, in Ireland, in Canada, in America, in Africa, in the Philippines and in various other countries. The early converts that remained in Greece make up the core of an ongoing international ministry that continues to thrive since its inception in 1976.

God led us from Greece to Germany, where we settled in 1991, just after the Berlin Wall came tumbling down. It is a point of interest that historic political changes occurred in both Greece and Germany just before arrived. We chose to live in a part of Germany where again there was not one apostolic believer. In this second phase of our missionary ministry, we have been able to start three churches and establish a number of other preaching points in uncharted German territory.

The strongest church started with an extended family of "GR" immigrants, including parents and three married children with their own young families, who started coming into the country in the same year that we were settling into our own life and ministry in the city of Bonn. We did not know them and they did not know God. God placed us, however, just three to four driving hours apart in northwestern Germany so that He could work from both ends and bring us all together with relative ease when the need arose. As Germans, they had the right to emigrate out of Kazakhstan and obtain immediate residency in Germany. Their quality of life improved immensely but everything was tainted by the escalating hold of drugs on the youngest married son. Our Lord, in His great mercy, stepped into their lives with deliverance and salvation, working first through a woman with a distant but clear connection to Andrew D. Urshan.

Digressing briefly back to the introduction of this book, remember that Andrew Urshan had embraced the Pentecostal message in America in the early 1900s. Once his Assyrian father learned that his eldest son had converted to a "strange" new religion abroad, he dispatched his next oldest son to America to straighten him out. Instead, the older persuaded the younger and Timothy received the Holy Ghost. The brothers returned to Iran in 1914 to present the message to their own people. A great outpouring of the Holy Ghost came upon the traditionally reserved Assyrians and hundreds were filled with the Spirit and baptized within a few months, including five members of the Urshan family.

While God was mightily at work, so were opposition forces, first from within and then from without. The Assyrian converts in Iran faced persecution from various other Christian groups and Andrew was threatened with deportation if they would not cease their evangelistic efforts. While these efforts failed, WWI broke out and a second enemy charged on the scene with brute force.

Kurdish and Turkish soldiers, under cover of the war effort, came flooding across the border into northern Iran intending to wipe out the minority Assyrian, Armenian and Greek Christian populations in the country. It was an extension of what they were already doing in Turkey. Waves of massacres occurred from 1914-1919. Andrew and his family were caught up in a time when people were brutally uprooted from their homes, suffered from raging diseases and were butchered by the thousands without cause. Andrew lost his passport and legal papers and typhus fever almost took his life. His mother died as the family fled from their home but the rest of the family, dad and the five Urshan brothers, managed to escape into Russia late in 1915.

During the nine months that the Urshan family spent in Russia, Andrew wasted no time in ministering the Gospel and, once again, people flocked to hear him preach. Some one hundred and eighty Russians were baptized and received the Holy Ghost in the dead of winter when ice had to be chopped away to accomplish the task! Andrew himself was baptized in Jesus' Name at that time. This astounding response occurred all the while Russia was experiencing its own time of trouble.[16] A revolution was brewing. Food was scarce and riots were abundant. The

---

[16] These conditions escalated into the Russian Revolution and would have been a factor in preventing the Reinhold Sass family from entering Russia a few years later as missionaries, had they gathered the funds to do so.

Urshans and many others who had fled from Iran realized that they were not safe in Russia either. Andrew and two brothers went on to America while their father and two other brothers returned to Iran. The believers left behind in Russia, who called themselves "Urshanites", were dispersed into far reaches of the vast former Soviet Union due to government persecution. Amazingly, they retained their apostolic faith through seventy years of communist rule that followed the Russian revolution.

Coming back to the German connection, we are ready to tie a knot that brings Iranian, American, Russian and German story strands together as only the Lord can do it. You see, the woman who came to Germany to rescue the troubled young man was both his mother-in-law and a member of an "Urshanite" church back home. She brought a lifeline of hope to her addicted son-in-law and he grabbed on to it just in time. Although she was prepared to take her daughter and grandchildren back home, she decided to give the Lord a chance to work first. Fortified by a period of fasting, she admonished her son-in-law to repent and he did! She informed him that the power of the Holy Ghost could bring salvation and deliverance and it did! All but one adult in his extended family repented after witnessing the deliverance of their son and brother. These new believers were filled with the Holy Ghost without a preacher in sight.

A family revival began among people who had never before heard of Pentecost. God had planted us in proximity so that we could baptize them, disciple them and help them establish churches in their cities. In the twelve years since we met this family, two dedicated and capable men, blood brothers, have accepted a call to preach and are pastoring two of the churches established together in northwestern Germany.

I find it amazing that the Urshan story thread would start its journey in Iran, go to America, then go back to Iran, weave its way through Russia and return to America, where it would intermingle with Auroraville and my life some years later, finally intertwining with bright new strands from Russia that would make their way into Germany to be woven right back into my own present life! Can God's handiwork get any more beautiful than this?

Oh, but, wait ... there are a few more strands being woven in from my side of the story. Although our three children shared in the extraordinary works of God around the world with us, they have chosen to enhance the beauty of the tapestry from America. Laura Demos Payne is the music pastor and administrative assistant in a U.P.C.I. church in Tennessee; Joel Alexander Demos is the assistant pastor in a U.P.C.I. church in Minnesota; Philip Alan Demos is the Youth Pastor in a U.P.C.I. church in Wisconsin. They and their families are striving with us to believe and to live in a way that brings honor to our spiritual forefathers and gives all the glory to God."

Appendix I

MAJOR EVENT CHRONOLOGY

- 1906   The Azusa Street revival begins in Los Angeles.
- 1915   Midway Tabernacle opens in St. Paul.
- 1918   The Carl Ebert family comes into Pentecost.
- 1919   Rosa Ebert Oelke embraces Pentecost.
- 1919-24   Rosa becomes a spiritual leader in Green Lake.
- 1920   Eau Claire Pentecostal Assembly incorporates.
- 1922   The Fred Lentz family comes into the faith.
- 1922-3   Preachers arrive and assist Rosa in Green Lake.
- 1924   The Oelke family moves to Eau Claire.
- 1924   A vacant Auroraville factory becomes a church.
- 1924   The Harrington family comes into Pentecost.
- 1925   Reinhold Sass becomes the first pastor.
- 1925   The first regional Ministers' Conference is held.
- 1926   *The Church at Auroraville* is destroyed by fire.
- 1926-8   A new church is built in Auroraville.
- 1927   Carl Ebert becomes the pastor.
- 1927-8   A church opens in Medford, Wisconsin.
- 1928   The new church building is officially dedicated.
- 1928   The Great Depression begins in America.
- 1928   The Gottlieb Hardt family comes into the faith.
- 1929   Jim and Marie Peterson come into the faith.
- 1930-1   A church opens in Clintonville, Wisconsin.
- 1934   Samuel Hardt and Sadie Harrington marry.
- 1937   Stuart G. Norris opens Apostolic Bible Institute.
- 1937-8   Samuel Hardt pastors *The Church at Auroraville*.
- 1941-5   U.S.A. military forces enter World War II.
- 1941   Richard Davis pastors *The Church at Auroraville*.
- 1946   *The Church at Auroraville* closes.

Appendix II

REFLECTIONS AND TRIBUTES

Those who experienced the wonder-working power of God in the early 1900s were too involved in making it happen to keep records. Samuel Hardt recalls that more than thirty converts were baptized in the spring of 1925 in Auroraville alone. We know that such events were repeated over and over again and every name is recorded in the Lamb's Book of Life. According to Scripture, we also know that even the very hairs of every head that was "dunked" in the old millpond are numbered!

This account of God's sovereign work through *The Church at Auroraville* is certainly incomplete but is the portion known from the facts left behind. It has been presented with as much accuracy as the contributors could ascertain and presented with great love and respect for the service our pioneering predecessors and their families so willingly and lovingly rendered.

Those of us whose spiritual life generates from the altar of *The Church at Auroraville* know first-hand how often and in what manner sacrifices were made. Those of you, our readers, who have likewise embraced Pentecost in other times and places likely have a host of pioneers in your personal histories that paid a great price to bring you into Pentecost. Perhaps this story, our story, will incite some of you to research and write your own chronicle. Our descendants should know that the legacies left by our pioneers in Pentecost are highly-valued by those of us who follow along behind their remarkable examples.

Rosa Ebert Oelke   [1884 – 1972]

"I remember visiting my Grandma Oelke in her apartment near downtown Eau Claire. She loved talking about the Bible and was an ardent defender of the Oneness to the very end. Examining scripture, plunging deep into Old Testament references and balancing them out with the New Testament was pure joy for her. Those early pioneers learned to discern truth, to sift and winnow through all the errors in teaching that came along. They gave up family members and friends but drew great strength from one another through encouraging letters. I have one of my grandma's well-worn Bibles, marked with her thoughts. She would be so pleased to know that, down to the sixth generation, she is not forgotten as we carry on in this precious Pentecostal Way!"

Mary Oelke Geissler, granddaughter
Pentecostal Assembly, Eau Claire, Wisconsin

Carl Frederick Ebert   [1881 – 1971]

"I was fortunate to have Carl F. Ebert as my grandfather. I credit his family visits to St. Louis for my desire to be saved. I loved and honored him so much that I even took my bride Jane to visit him on our honeymoon. Thankfully, I was able to hear him preach several times and one message that comes to mind was preached when he was in his 80s. It was around Christmas time and he talked about gifts that are usually wrapped. In order to get the gift, the wrapping has to be torn. Likewise, in order for us to receive the gift of the Holy Ghost, the body of Jesus had to be torn at Calvary. Grandfather Ebert modeled Jesus Christ before me. "

Dr. Arlo Ebert Moehlenpah, grandson
U.P.C.I. Licensed Minister, Poway, CA

A final note from Jon:

Most members of *The Church at Auroraville* have gone on to their just rewards. Few wrote down details garnered from their unique perspectives about how this vigorous church developed. Fortunately, some can still speak of those early times and we acknowledge them here.

- Esther Lentz Haskins, daughter of Fred and Pauline Lentz
- Eunice Ebert Glenna, daughter of Carl and Martha Ebert
- LaVerne Sass Monte, daughter of Reinhold and Lydia Sass
- Lee Harrington, uncle to Jon Hardt
- Samuel Hardt, father to Jon Hardt
- John Peterson, son of Jim and Marie Peterson
- Donna Kirk, Auroraville historian who provided photos

The people listed above were invaluable in answering questions and providing the story content, dates and names that fill these pages. There is another list of folks who contributed ideas and opinions as the story unfolded. They are not listed here. Nevertheless, they are very much appreciated and they know who they are! What was common to all was an agreement that this story must be told. We thank every person who participated in preparing this material to go into print.

The Church in Auroraville story might never have been recorded had I not stopped by to visit Esther Haskins one day to look at her photo collection. I was interested in finding pictures of Esther and my mother, Sadie Harrington Hardt, who grew up together. As Esther was identifying people in various photos in relation to my mother, her family and *The Church at Auroraville*, she began to tell a story that took me greatly by surprise in its scope and its influence on my own life.

Jon Hardt and Esther Haskins, selecting photos for this book
Esther, here in 2009, at 96 years young

I did not find photos of my mother but found an interesting and important story that I concluded others, like myself, in succeeding generations, would find relevant. At first, I thought I could record this story in four or five pages that would serve as an inspirational insert in church newsletters. As you now know, a chance encounter at Esther Lentz Haskins' kitchen table evolved into a story that is much bigger than any of us realized at the outset.

Now that the story has been told, it is clear that our pioneers exhibited a level of dedication that we should strive to match. They brought the message of Pentecost out of obscurity and into the light. The endearing and enduring aspect of Rosa Oelke's witness is simply that she did her utmost to share the Gospel in her time and in her place and in her way.

She lived it before family, friends and neighbors, delivering the message so effectively that the good news seemed to reach everyone in her pathway! Her example does inspire us in our time to do the same.

I was born on the Harrington farm just outside of Auroraville, firstborn of Samuel and Sadie Harrington Hardt, and would become one in a long line of Auroraville preachers' kids when my parents returned there to pastor in the late 1930s. Over the years, I have met others with similar life experiences and we all seem to view our roots with pride. It has been my privilege to tell this story on behalf of all the others whose lives have been shaped similarly as mine.

We who can trace our beginnings to *The Church at Auroraville* have a well-earned camaraderie. We feel blessed by this linkage and wear our badges gladly, realizing that our ancestors paid a great price to pass the torch on to us. They will be thanked properly and profusely on that distant shore!

Jon Hardt
Author

A last word from Valerie:

I was born into the Tesmer-Thieme family in 1942, born-again in 1959 and married in 1970. We went off to far away places starting in 1973. A missionary appointment in 1974 with the U.P.C.I. put us on a path that we each knew from the time of our late teens was designed for us.

Alan and I were gifted with rich apostolic heritages that came through family or divinely directed associations. We had always valued these enhancements to our lives but never so much as now. When Jon's book project came along and completely pulled me in, a deeper understanding came my way. I thank you, Jon, with all my heart, for this splendid opportunity

Alan and Valerie Demos
U.P.C.I. Missionaries to Germany

to share in getting your story, my story and, most importantly, the story of our pioneers into print.

It has been a great pleasure to live in Germany, to date, for almost twenty years, with the expressed purpose of bringing the Gospel to German-speaking people. I thank God for my dear and dedicated husband, whose calling, vision and tenacity have taken me to places around the world where the echo of that tiny village of Auroraville is still ringing and bringing people to their knees.

Valerie Ann Demos
Editor

Now, we see it is dusk
at the old millpond,
a time to pause,
reflect
and give thanks.

By the way,
would you care to go fishing?

The Auroraville Fishers of Men
would be so pleased
to have you join them.